# A TABLE OF CONTENT

# A Table of Content

*Poems*

## DOROTHEA TANNING

*Graywolf Press*

Publication of this volume is made possible in part by a grant provided by the Minnesota State Arts Board, through an appropriation by the Minnesota State Legislature; a grant from the Wells Fargo Foundation Minnesota; and a grant from the National Endowment for the Arts, which believes that a great nation deserves great art. Significant support has also been provided by the Bush Foundation; Target, Marshall Field's and Mervyn's with support from the Target Foundation; the McKnight Foundation; and other generous contributions from foundations, corporations, and individuals. To these organizations and individuals we offer our heartfelt thanks.

Special funding for this title has been provided by the Jerome Foundation.

Published by Graywolf Press
250 Third Avenue North, Suite 600
Minneapolis, Minnesota 55104
All rights reserved.

www.graywolfpress.org

Published in the United States of America

ISBN 978-1-55597-402-2

2 4 6 8 9 7 5 3

Library of Congress Control Number: 2003112162

Cover collage: Dorothea Tanning, *Encyclopedia* (detail), 1990
Cover design: Julie Metz

# ACKNOWLEDGMENTS

Acknowledgments are due to the editors of the following magazines where some of these poems first appeared:

"Are You?" and "Pursued, I Ran into the Barn" — *LIT*

"Aspects of Ice, Detail," "Heaven on Earth," "Il a Trouvé la Mort," "Landscape with Postmark," and "Rain of Blood, Aix-en-Provence" — *The Gettysburg Review*

"Awake at Fifteen," "Sybaris," and "Two City Mice" — *Western Humanities Review*"

"Collage *(La Femme 100 Têtes)*" — *Literary Imagination*

"Destinations," "Figure Approaching, Opposite," and "Secret" — *The New Yorker*

"End of the Day on Second," "Graduation," and "Time Flew" — *Antioch Review*

"Flea Market (Rainy Day)," "Fortune Cookies," and "9 table settings" — *Boston Review*

"Flea Market (Rainy Day)," "Landscape with Postmark," "9 table settings," "Report from the Field," and "Rue Monge Narrated" also appeared in *American Poet: The Journal of The Academy of American Poets.*

"Insomnia, my cousin" and "Report from the Field" — *The Paris Review*

"Life of Crime: St. Julien le Pauvre" — *Partisan Review*

"No Palms" and "Unfounded Certitudes" — *The Yale Review*

"No Palms" also appeared in *Best American Poetry 2000.*

"Of Flesh and Gold" and "The Triumph of Venus" — *SOLO*

"Orphanotrophium" — *The New Republic*

"Reckless Words" and "Strawberries" — *Southwest Review*

"Rue Monge Narrated" and "To Zeno" — *Ploughshares*

"Sequestrienne" — *Poetry*

"Waverly and a Place" — *Parnassus*

# POEMS

## I

Are You?   3
Aspects of Ice, Detail   5
A Table of Content   6
Awake at Fifteen   7
Bridge, Moon, Professor, Shoes   8
Camouflage   9
Collage *(La Femme 100 Têtes)*   12
Destinations   14
End of the Day on Second   15
Figure Approaching, Opposite   16
Flea Market (Rainy Day)   18
Fortune Cookies   19
Graduation   20

## II

Heaven on Earth   23
Il a Trouvé la Mort   25
Insomnia, my cousin,   27
It's Late in the Rue de Lille   28
Landscape with Postmark   30
Life of Crime: St. Julien le Pauvre   32
Minor Incident at the Intersection   35
9 table settings   36
No Palms   37
Occupied Musical Chairs   38

Of Beatitude  40
Of Flesh and Gold  42
Orphanotrophium  43

# III

Pursued, I Ran into the Barn  47
Raft  48
Rain of Blood, Aix-en-Provence  50
Reckless Words  52
Reminders  53
Report from the Field  54
Rue Monge Narrated  55
Secret  57
Sequestrienne  58
Sibylline  59
Six Avian Perils  60
Space Disarmed  64
Strawberries  65
Sybaris  67

# IV

The Triumph of Venus  71
This Is a Recording  72
Time Flew  73
To Our Father Who Art  74
To That Garden  75
Tour Dynamics  76
To Zeno  78
Two City Mice  79
Unfounded Certitudes  80
Waverly and a Place  81
Window Treatment  83

*It's hard to be always the same person.*   MONTAIGNE

# I

---

## A to G

# ARE YOU?

If an expatriate is, as I believe, someone
who never forgets for an instant
being one,
then, no.

But, if knowing that you always
tote your country around
with you, your roots,
a lump

like a soul that will never leave you
stranded in alien subsets of
yourself, or your wild
entire;

that being elsewhere packs a vertigo,
a tightrope side you cannot
pass up, another way
to show

how not to break your pretty neck
falling on skylights:
reward-laden
mirages;

then, yes. All homes are home; mirages
everywhere. Aside from
gravity, there are no
limits,

never were, nor will there ever be,
no here and there to foil
your lotus-dreaming
legend.

Stay on the planet, if you can. It isn't
all that chilly and what's more,
grows warmer by the
minute.

# ASPECTS OF ICE, DETAIL

The chalky blur of failed snapshots defines my father's landscape:
too dim, in our opinion, too inexistent — we too young.

And yet, he gravely dwells there, tells its distant details,
his face behind his fingers as though their interstices saw elsewhere,

saw endless night in daytime, snow-pall like suffocation,
saw how woolen weight of sky leaned into basalt outcroppings

as if to drop its blanket over their naked thrusting.
No birds disturb the stasis, silence feeds the pewter lake.

And something about a wolf or what must have been one,
now flattened, freeze-framed, a fur rug for praying, a prayer rug.

Details. My father, too, is at these times as distant as his landscape,
skating home on ice we try to believe in. Thin ice.

My mother has no landscape. She doesn't seem to need one,
listening to the details, explicit as Scandinavia, respectfully.

Opening her icebox door — "Don't say icebox, say fridge" —
she contemplates its bounty, its beautifully labeled nourriture:

Marmalade's senoritas rustle lampshade flounces. Olives,
cola, Queen Anne maraschinos that my mother sees and doesn't.

She feels a rabid breathing slide down along her spine
as Andy, skating fast, heads home, wherever that is — poor Andy!

And all this summer evening, immense in its magnanimity,
blackens to deepest rue. She wonders what she came for, shivering

before her icebox maw, its sour cream and half-and-half
sinisterly disappearing under filthy snowdrifts and dead wolves.

# A TABLE OF CONTENT

On pale cloth, artistically arranged
musical objects
(she used to sing):
a mandolin, bottom up,
a crumpled score,
(if played he might not like it),
a pile of books
in disrespectful disarray.
Tablemap.
A lighted lamp.
White grapes.

*Class adjourned. Quietude clings like tedium,*
*pulsing green and*
*coiled around him,*
*vinelike.*
*He thinks he likes it*
*on the classroom table*
*of multiplication*
*eating purple grapes.*
*Lessons aside.*
*Muffled cries, heard, unheard.*
*He thinks he likes it.*

Moving object, bottle-shaped,
rising topaz bubbles.
Why wait?

*Wait. . . .*

## AWAKE AT FIFTEEN

Once intended for a long voyage
my palanquin broke down.
Witnesses remember nothing;
nor I, as all begins again,
as space
        slows to a
                    standstill —

    it's Zeno, streaking, nearly colliding
    with Venus, warm-hearted planet.
    (She has a husband who all but left,
    her lovingkindness too much for him.)

Back home with my flowers. I'm wide awake
and going nowhere.

    Daddy says to watch me like a hawk.
    You see I have these brain emissions,
    spattered sounds under the bridge.

    What was it —
        petals dropping on the floor,
                   on the tiles,

    death tapping a rose on the shoulder
    in the maelstrom night?

Just imagine, I have a lover.

# BRIDGE, MOON, PROFESSOR, SHOES

Slept dreams, they say, take just a few seconds
no matter how long they are. Or how far

I walked on that bridge of spider silk
with the moon beside me like a friend.

Her light trapped us in a radiance of bliss so
pure, hours weren't hours, or minutes minutes

as we passed my old lecture hall, its professor
stopping in the middle of his question "Can

someone here tell me — ?" to stare at us as we
floated along, my insouciance blurring a little

with a sense of guilt. Had I a right to this?
Could such joy be mine for free? If I had

a purpose — say, shoes. Find shoes. On earth
we don't walk on air — not like this windless

void riding underfoot, its force backing me
into the immensities, their black nowhere.

Such bouncing's tiresome. Where's the bliss?
The moon reaches for my arm. I jerk away.

What a pie-face she is in her chalky pallor.
Why did that professor turn his back on me?

Oh, if I find shoes (size seven) they won't be
on too soon to get me home, home    home.

# CAMOUFLAGE

### 1

Unmarked lanes, fog, spindrift.
They helped me lose my way back

to the time of not caring less and
burnt leaves from three poplar trees.

I leaned into my shadow and it leaned
into me. Little disappearances ensued.

As morning swallows dew, my shadow
swallowed what was left of morning,

struck out with me, our veil intact.
Oh, we were primed like canvas.

### 2

To get from there to here is a
long way past the Golden Horn.

To taste of ecstasy, drink its bitterness
are chances to take, blindfold games.

What is ordained if not the body's
piercing, its thorn and petal, sign

and symbol misunderstood? What is
conquest but the germ of capitulation?

My sign gave me a winning number.
It burned my hand before I saw it.

### 3

Clotted in drawing rooms — rooms
to draw the act through its last scene,

cozy imperatives forgot themselves,
froze and faltered in the wings.

My shadow watched the curtain fall
on what had been, would be again:

part rebellion, part saliva, formulaic.
To say I was there is to be a fossil

in an unnatural history museum,
acquisition number on my brow.

### 4

Camouflage as an indulgence
eats away what it thinks to hide.

Amateur for ways of seeing
I dally with the hard-to-get,

wanting at last to get things
straight and all of a piece.

### 5

If the Golden Horn still gleams
over there in its dolent splendor;

if it still blows sweet barcaroles
and liquid sighs, they're not for me.

My boat sails an unmapped route,
slips through keyhole and custom,

churns upriver to bring me back
to where, in truth, I never was.

Shadowy, my shadow leads the way
as I step on board in my traveling

cloak, trailing a scarf of history in case
of weather and nothing to read.

# COLLAGE *(La Femme 100 Têtes)*

*(for M.E.)*


A studio afternoon.
Down left with you, at table chaos
bidden and unbidden, it's all the same
under your hand: germinal,
clotted dust, mosaic tribes, an island night,

                                      riven.


Beyond the window, rain.


A two-dimensional leopard wrapped in instinct
loves herself alone. You carve her out of paper,

                                     out of context.
Glue thickens like a plot.


Conjured scenario: scissor scheme explodes.
How else to float your favorite chair
among the waves, then sit in it?
Your cut-and-paste deny this play
where chapters strew the floor like sand.

A door somewhere unfolds.


Perturbation, your sister, reaches for your hand,
*the hundred headless woman opens her august sleeve.*
It all comes together, breathing itself

                              into shapeliness.

Abashed, our turmoil drips.
Your plunder is the code,
the reason for this day of rain,
for all things unbelievable    believed.

## DESTINATIONS

Yesterday I saw some bears at the top of a waterfall.
They were watching salmon leap up from the cascade.

It was on television and, moreover, part of an ad.
Not one of them, salmon or bears, was impressed

by the water's will, its weight, its wrath, its wall,
the salmon flying out from that knockout force

like careless birds rising from a field of silver wheat.
The falling water obviously had no intention of getting

in the way of a salmon's destination. It was beautiful.
Trouble was, the bears were there with bear intentions.

Their heads bobbed up and down, perhaps admiring
every quiver and flash, their four feet as firmly planted

in water as the rock-face itself. Now and then one of them
opened its mouth to let a fish dive into it. That was the part

that made me think of my own headlong leaps and dives
when I thought there would be no mouths to receive me.

# END OF THE DAY ON SECOND

Her husband, traveling for his company, is rarely home.
Alone, she keeps herself to herself except for the stores.

Once past their revolving doors those mouse-gray webs
of thought that hang around her head like crape soon

lose their grayness, give way to garlands of things, new
things, needed things. She is quick of step, clear of eye,

purposeful. Seven floors of exhilaration await her.
Escalator-bound, she hardly pauses to touch a faux-fur

something which, like all else blazing in its newness, urges
invitation from every counter, every aisle: "Touch me,

open me, feel me, turn me over, unzip me, try me on,
read my label, my price tag, touch me, oh touch me. . . ."

Finally, on second, in bras. Bras swarming everywhere,
giant pink moths at rest, empty cups clamoring,

"Fill me." It's late. Shoppers have left, yet there's time
to try a bra. Emerging from the booth she stands, only

half-dressed and head down, in aisle five, a bra hanging
from her hand. A floorwalker approaches. "May I help you?"

She doesn't look up, murmurs, "My husband is away."
At this, the kindly floorwalker takes her in his arms, her

face hidden on his shoulder. They stand, unmoving,
among the mothy bras that might at any moment rise

in a cloud and leave them, as I am leaving them now,
in their frozen pose, their endless closing time.

# FIGURE APPROACHING, OPPOSITE

It was someone I knew, had known in one of those lives
somewhere but where it was whispering so fast I needed time;

not sure, and yet a girl-shape so like Nina — just thinking of Nina
was a smile spreading along my spine — although of course it

couldn't be Nina: so in a hurry high heels tapping on pavement,
arms hugging a plastic bundle, yes, Nina's moon-face under a shag.

If this was now, Nina back then, how far back might be only last year
when events had begun to take their toll on her imperturbability,

cramped her style, if style it was, wearing no makeup with jeans
that always turned out to be Claire's. Closer now I see it's not Nina

but Claire, the only one we called reasonable, trying to keep Nina
from ruining Kevin's life (and her own), Claire holding up Jenny as

a model of happy union with Rick; she believed it until the night
Jenny was found slashed and comatose in the bathtub, lovely Jenny

giving all she had in the world to promote Rick's so-called career
in that dedicated way Claire so loved, not realizing it was Jenny

herself she loved — or was it Nina — but wanting them all to succeed
in spite of rent and the violence that sent Jenny to her, tender Jenny

but transparent — Claire could see right through Jenny if she danced
in front of light and fast as if there might be other dances waiting

to be danced; that was Jenny and here she comes, it's Jenny not Claire,
I might have known, Jenny now working in some convenience store,

its logo half-visible on the bag clutched to her chest. I open my mouth to
say Hi, the bundle snorts at me from a dripping snout between red eyes

while Jenny's stare shoves the void in my gaping mouth that I close
barely in time to see that it wasn't Jenny after all, nor was it Claire

or even Nina, just someone with a bundle of virulent Convenience,
behind me now, my grateful breathing glad she did not know me.

# FLEA MARKET (RAINY DAY)

Get out of the car. Walk into. Look a web-sited spider in the eye
as she burnishes her mood and marquetry. T-shirts wilt nearby.

Picnicking through lace and bombazine she'll think wineglass
or Babylonian baby-face, pre-cast. Forgive her table for teethmarks.

Photography was invented in eighteen hundred and some proofs.
Pick up the leprous postcard: Samarkand or is it Tashkent? Hand-tinted

bluedomes spatter across the alley, sink in a last sunspot. Eiffel Tower
made of toothpicks, out of a story, out of a lifetime, if only I had made it —

Head in the clouds matching weather. Mindlessness lasting till noon.
Open a dog-eared treatise. It seems the gorilla was the first biped

to introduce lineage measure, basing his elegant reasoning on the notion
of reversal of dominance — it's sprinkling — form, indeed, a regression.

Dry me. Dry the mirror softly and she will not waken there, only don't
look back, you'll see no wearer for bracelets' tinny bangles braiding

small sound on rain-dropped picture frames gaping for lost walls,
and Hyacinth Rigaud who in chromolithography here paints his king.

Put your ear to our brain-dead clock, house and home of fleas. Tireless,
their little thuds mark time, the hours, the patina like ours. Let them

hold this summer's trance in water made of rain. No door to slam,
tarpaulins come out. Watch your step. Get the mirror into the car.

# FORTUNE COOKIES

Blackwidow and bluedaughter will precede a bronze fortune. Wait ninety-one dawns.

Try aulic apples and eco-similes when up a tree. On the next moon's round you will hear a new note.

A fixed star burns the edges of frayed identity. Look underground for knockout denouement.

Swarming doubt surrounds your final forfeit. Your aura is now in orbit. Wear its disguise.

Learn the Erynnian language of thorns. Make a pact with chaos. From then on you won't care.

The faces in the mirror have learned to talk. If you listen they will slash your past, ignite your future.

In ten days your eyes will see a glaive. Take it as a sign of promise. Your beauty will explode.

Mix wine with semen and ectoplasm. Throw it out. You shall be richly rewarded.

Wild rapture spins over your personal landscape. Do not hold your breath in the fire. This sign is bliss.

Entrance to Hell demands grit. After nine days in the ashes you will be walking on air.

Go mad and you will not become truly insane. Tomorrow you will be chosen.

# GRADUATION

He told us, *with the years, you will come*
*to love the world.*
And we sat there with our souls in our laps,
and comforted them.

# II

H to O

# HEAVEN ON EARTH

pronounced in a phone booth long-distance from a friend
who doesn't see the havoc she invites by bringing in

without visa and safe-conduct (much less a real identity),
a somewhere or is it something to take up room though

there is none available — the hotel booked solid and
the beach restricted — yet she is certain Heaven's there

to make Earth attractive and well worth the money
forked over to her travel agent for the ten-day package;

all of it redounding on the innocent developers' having
made their dearly paid-for property too, well, heavenly,

never dreaming it would be confronted by an alien invasion
of the most insidious kind that only lawyers called upon

to argue deeds of ownership and especially to question
the need of Heaven to render Earth agreeable can deal with.


Gazing from the beach my friend might see fishing tubs
out early in the glint and heave of water, clearly
neither on Earth or in Heaven but just casting nets

that should be full by noon or else a lot of people
in the shacks up on the hill will face a nothing meal.
Some days the fish don't bite or swarm into the nets,

just swim and flash and dive, and on those days
the fishermen are not so likely to sing and clown
around: they pull the boats in silence up on sand,

the suck of it holding feet to itself, Earth holding
them close, close to the mud hill, mud house, the big
banana leaf laden tonight with frijoles, fish or no fish,

the stars safely sewn into their velvet profundities
and somebody with his guitar next door making Earth
sounds and love sounds that know no other Heaven.

# IL A TROUVÉ LA MORT

In French death is feminine,
A sort of mother or sister,
Someone you had lost track of,
Almost forgotten about.
Years and years gone by
Without a sign from her.
Nothing but her artful way
Of not forgetting you.

Dressed in bones, la Mort
Is still depicted as
A male without a member —
Necessarily, since *verge*
Is resolutely girlish
And not to be confused
With hers, a boyish one
(Thus proving her authority).

The sexes! Ever playful or
Dead serious? Could it be
That hers, being masculine,
Guides entry lined with maleness
To a shy but comely guest
Who's not altogether sure
She-he wants to go there?
It's all so equivocal.

Maybe for the French
Such a mix-up lays to rest
Once and for all old notions
Of who's who, what goes where.
It's clear their language begs
The question charmingly

If not for us, for them,
And ferrets out this fact:

Neither him nor her,
The goddess-god, delicately
Playing hide-and-seek
In order to surprise
Is only death, la Mort,
Who makes no promises
Except sometimes to be there
Across the street — see her?

# INSOMNIA, MY COUSIN,

you ride the night machine
witlessly in bedlam,
breathing on my screen,
my panting outdoor movie,
its paid admission being
my square root,
my flashbulb
socket-pinned and joyless.

Insomnia, my cousin,
you have sired nightly
indecent vertigo.
I lie haggard as you drag
your insane engine past
across the floor,
slamming doors
on all my four dimensions,

leaving me high day
to shred the clotted dream.
Cousin, I repeatedly
betray you with its debris.

# IT'S LATE IN THE RUE DE LILLE

*(April 1st, 1976)*

It's always too late to keep in mind
who not to invite next time,
                    even if they've all

left for the time being,
time being no match
                    for this time-killing room
                    turning blue,
happening slow to happen
and we in our time-killing
                    vapory avatars.

To challenge the labyrinth's
veil-hung night; to go on
                    spinning our web —

oh, it would have been
no more than our right,
                    not his, the One
                    sitting there —

Who invited him, anyway? —
so hollow-eyed, bony,
                    and all out of tune

with that mouthful of piano keys.
Did he forget to leave?
                    Should I say
                    something — ?

"Can't you see
someone's tired here. . .
                    not too well, in fact?"

He — it — grins, says nothing,
with an air of imminence
                    that falls
                    like black snow

on the room, on the man
in its bed, and on
                    killed time.

# LANDSCAPE WITH POSTMARK

### 1

On that plain of sand and wind in March.
                              Or no — it's an illusion.
                              Try names:
Blad al Hamra, Amazigh, El Mo'izz. No use.

Here is a nowhere, a waste, a thrust-up slab of stone,
          a speck in vastness,
          in eternal wind,
          in a sickening solitude
                              of African blaze

until the sweet mirage, billowing black
          and real in the shimmer:
                              *"Je peux vous aider?"*

Her Berber face as slow, as graven
          as Araby itself,
          factual as the brow tattoo,
          the thirsty eyes that drained mine
          or would have drained them
                              of their blurred falter.

Two women scarved in ambiguity of wind,
          we share the slab,
          our words blown like sand from mouth to ear
          and back to mouth in a tongue neither
          hers nor mine, waiting
          not for my tarrying friends,
                              but for
                              something
          that could never happen, there
                              or anywhere in this world.

## 2

Her letters: drowning messages in bottles
  of desert-stricken glass (we all know
  it turns to amethyst).

What can I do? Kabira!
  Did you get the shortwave radio?
      Do you still live
  at Derb Amzmiz,
  Kasbah, Marrakech?

# LIFE OF CRIME: ST. JULIEN LE PAUVRE

In awe and transport what pregnant queen would not
hold dear the augur's words, "Your son will be a saint"?
She told no one.

The boy galloped his horse beside his father.
"Some day you will be king." Kneeling on Sunday
after Sunday in chapel,

watching the mouse by his hole in the wall
and bored, bored; idly, with his little sword
he severed its nose

and the drop of blood was a drunken ocean, red
without anger, red without even lust, a blindness
of dawn to scarlet

sunset, a birth of death spiraling down
with the castle's doves to moat and muck, a kind
of childish prologue

to the man's arrows, darts, knives, javelins aimed
at everything that moved and would move no more
in forest and desert.

What breathlessness, what sluicing ecstasy
in the red flowing from feather from fur from skin
from eye socket!

Did he taste the red salt in his own red gullet?
Did the martyred beast and plummeted bird ravish
his austere will?

Each time, oh, each time with each convulsion
it was as if he slavered like a Cerberus obeying
an implacable master

of carnage in The Peaceable Kingdom, felled
one by one with their death throes, their agonies.
Until the black stag,

an arrow quivering between his eyes, cried out:
"Accursed one. You will murder your mother
and your father."

Shaken, trembling a little he fled, traveled far.
Such a curse was not to be taken lightly
even by an assassin

though for a time slaughter was human: a needful
expedient to fulfill the promise of kingship,
and long enough

for the old blood-craze to stain the way into
the last prophecy: one of those bedroom spasms
of domestic confusion.

From pink-nosed mouse to murder of mother
and father, a tapestry of death strewn in between,
was far enough

in depravity to confirm not royal grandeur
but time for heavenly judgment. He reversed
the situation

by dressing for holiness. Ah, it is too bad, Flaubert,
even in deadpan irony, that you should speak
of penitence,

lampoon the cowl. And you, Julien, your travesty
of grace — another prideful posture, though bloodless
this time;

or more truly a ploy — your show of tears, your
eyes revulsed, your sores your filth your empty
begging bowl.

Warm the leper. Embrace him, mouth to mouth.
Now reveal the deal, the plea bargain you made
with God.

# MINOR INCIDENT AT THE INTERSECTION

This morning's paste defines itself as rain,
tells me to stay home. I wish I could.

If only I didn't have to prove something
no one will believe until I've proved it.

Outside, habit eats the day, already stale
with future relics. I corner my resolve

as mind-tattered pieces of me splinter
off the intersection, roll under traffic —

naked bits of purpose smashed under
cars, fire trucks, buses. Worse, this flying

among the citizenry should be reported.
Red, green, red, aping each other, as one,

proving nothing, leaving it up to me.
What is naked all about — fur or no fur?

*Let go of me. What are you doing?*
*What red light? No Yes. No. I have to*

*prove something. You don't understand.*
*Let me — I can prove it, if you — oh, go away . . .*

Red and green fur in my mouth. Green
bodies with red faces oozing like lava.

*No, not that. Of course I know my name.*
*No, nothing. I told them . . . told them . . .*

# 9 TABLE SETTINGS

candle flame
someone gasps behind
red fingers

courtly guests
hang out the window
killing time

tidals wave
without a drop of
rain or wine

on a fork
in her river slide
a few fish

below the
salt someone's career
sounds like glass

no time to
duel with crumbs and
cutlery

tonight melts
ice in draped glances
oh meringue

in spite of
tablescape I am
not my hand

finally
conscience is silent
as a plate.

## NO PALMS

No palms dolled up the tedium, no breathing wind.
No problem was the buzzword then, their way to go.

In truth, my case was black as sin, a thing to hide,
In that they feigned to find me sane, so not to know.

Someone brought in a medium. Anathema!
Some clown sewed up my eyes, he said it wouldn't show.

Confusing hands with craze, they howled, "Let's cut them off."
Confusing, too, their spies, my lies without an echo.

Time and again they stitched my mind with warp and woof.
Time pounded in my ruby heart, doing a slow,

Slow dim-out in that lupanar, slow take, slow fade,
Slow yawning like a door. "Hello," I said. "HELLO."

There, flung across the room between inside and out,
There must have shown itself to me . . . an afterglow.

With such a blaze to celebrate where centuries meet
With time itself, how could I hesitate? Although

Still trapped in the millennium I knew I had
Still time to blow some kisses. Look up, there they go!

# OCCUPIED MUSICAL CHAIRS

On Wolfgang, "the last real European," amalgam of all sweet sound,
flooding air with airs surely charmed from the very heavens,
laurels were scratchy and tended to fall off.

––––––––––

Laughing, he left the throne of fame, like fortune, empty.

––––––––––

Not for long. Ludwig, loomed, thundering *Vaterland,*
panic for chords, celestial choir —
                        crescendos striking close enough
to bring terminal silence —

––––––––––

                as out of the brick wall
                students came, swilling
                symphonic beer, worshipful
                *prosits* for Johannes, Vienna's
                winner of heavy medals.

––––––––––

Hiatus and a weather change came with mythic Richard.

Ancient thunder tore his ears apart, fold after fold;
tore into the core of him. His dawning need
sat on him like monolithic stone.

Its mute command
drove him from all he knew of wise restraint —
oh, so far from where he was, his other selves.
Soon he did not know them, nor they him.

———————

Of the end of things he made his sound.

———————

Dreams were crowded and contentious:
                              "All pasts are dim,"
he retorted, opening the piano to step inside.
By morning he had found the key:

———————

          *The only race that dared to kill off its gods.*

———————

                    He turned to courtly love
                    and *the ship drave on,*
                    as Cornwall hove.

———————

Exalted, he became The Holy Fool . . . Not quite.
Sounds were what he could make, notes of
grave and ancient thunder, and of his need
to seize the world, to open it,
to pour its fire in a cup.

# OF BEATITUDE

Out of pure habit the driest of mouths will not cry out. Desolate,
hers was of this kind.
Her cat was known to lie down with the mouse but wouldn't go
out to buy its cheese.
On summer evenings they sat in the garden where the drowning
sun reddened their faces.

She held the cat on her lap and rocked the mouse on her foot,
trying not to scream.
One day the postman delivered a package of cheese, but it
was the wrong kind.
In no time the mouse sickened and died, leaving nothing but
memories of dexterity.

With no one left to untangle her hair and that of the cat,
disorder reigned.
Matted tatters hung from couch and curtain, woman and cat.
Neighbors complained
of her wild garden, smelling of Venus flytrap, outlawed in
that monitored vicinity.

Mesmerized by watching flies succumb to Venus, she failed
to realize her cat mourned
the dead mouse; sitting alone at the far end of the garden,
gazing at the round red sun.
She didn't try to guess its thoughts, numbly aware they were
not sociable. Especially when,

despite her entreaties, it refused to translate for her when
she chatted with the trees.
Now, there were two monologues: her confidences and
the trees' leafy whispers,
becoming urgent and full of warning at night, laughing
at her in the morning.

A gardener came by looking for work. He hybridized exotic
plants and gave them the names
of his relatives: Alcibades, Prometheus, Titus Andronicus,
or of their dogs Zenon, Orfeo . . . .
Sunsets were rubicund and regular. Before long he was
sharing her bed, but did nothing

to help untangle her hair, maddeningly infested with midges.
She tried not to scream.
Her relationship with the cat had so deteriorated that it wouldn't
eat in her presence. That hurt.
And something was happening in the garden, with a fresh bud
turning black every night.

She suspected the plants' names were not those of the gardener's
relatives, nor of their dogs.
It all smelled of the classroom. Sure he had lied, she bade him sleep
thenceforth in the toolshed.
He folded his two extra undershirts, laid them in his knapsack,
and walked away down the road.

They still talk about her, how one evening she smashed all her
windows, trampled the Orfeos,
the Alcibades, even her precious Venus flytraps and caught
the last bus into town.
There, hairstyles are careful, and lifestyles meaningful. The cat has
a new mouse for evenings in the garden.

## OF FLESH AND GOLD

They swoon in the sun,
Pulchritudinous girls, boys.
Inside a door yawns.

At these rites the moon
Trembles and, worse, disappears
Without an excuse.

Body and face drift
Down with nightfall, unnoticed.
Draw near, draw nearer

Your destination.
Arriving bates a saved breath,
If that's the answer.

You always want more
Of the mire that lacerates.
Your veil is sulphur.

Slice a meteor
One bite of its transparence
Most satisfying

Down there in the blue
It didn't really happen:
Sexuality!

Sometimes in screaming
Echo fell silent as stone.
Yes, she lied she lied.

Death on a weekend
Opened the dance like a vein
Flaming flesh and gold.

# ORPHANOTROPHIUM

Six o'clock and the sky still there.
A little life at bay on the stairway,
   a lesson in white with some red
   added for conduct disorderly —

   according to matrons and patrons.

No schoolbook says a piece of ice
can scrape and slit bloodlessly
   through secondhand words we wear
   regardless of tongue and tie.

   Then how to speak languages fluently?

A tilt of the head to separate
the lung from all the colored marbles
   in the mouth will cover your tracks,
   blow dust in the courtyard.

# III

P to S

# PURSUED, I RAN INTO THE BARN

Rough-hewn shadows streamed around us,

Eyeless-seeming.

With hideous intent the pursuer came on,

Mindless, sniffing.

No stratagem, no swiftness would hide you,

Guileless and bleeding.

You were a bundle of fur in my arms,

Helpless, trusting.


Among barn-dwellers I sought concealment.

Shaftless, brushing

Away from the window I watched it come on,

Pitiless, secreting

Revenge from below. The insane thing,

Spineless, dripping,

Had already closed in. You stirred in my arms,

Weightless, leading

Me on to discover the end of the scheme,

The tearing sound in this poem's dream.

# RAFT

You were immense. You led me to the edge. I waved
      and we went over — I held my happy breath.
      We knew our raft would get us past the mountain.

Instead of sails we had the beating of our wings.
      They synthesized the savagery of sound and
      wove impulsive flights around our sphere.

Why was it, now, all over? Not prodigals, slipping
      home to hang our tragedy on the bedpost,
      we kept our part of the bargain, unimpressed

by alien dust. We peeled our eyes, cocked our
      ears, stayed near the beachhead, in case.
      Our flare: the corner of your gelatin-blue eye.

We saw great implications in the simplest geography
      and computed with the errancy of wind —
      its breath as quick in folly's fever as was ours

until surprise no longer held an element. It was in
      that slow light I saw where things were leading.
      Oh, it wasn't long before you were past caring.

Some undertow had opened, pulled you from me
      far beyond the beating of our wings
      into rare dark I had not known, nor know.

My silhouette, caved in, beds with transparency.
      Too dry for the alcove, too far from out there,
      slowly, now, I move in another skin.

Behind me night, equivocal with evidence:
  inky impetuosities swarm in the tattoos,
  a beached plane pretending to be a craft

just in from a mission leaks its cargo of tsetses.
  Farther down, several crows pick worms
  from massed driftwood. It looks like our raft.

# RAIN OF BLOOD, AIX-EN-PROVENCE

Toward noon, July 1608.
No light, or hardly. Hebetude lay
like a membrane on cobbles
and casseroles, on bread dough

                  like sin itself

in halfhearted concupiscence
with saturated time, conjuring
the stroke of noon, gleeful enemy
of toil, before the *coup de rouge.*

               A drop fell.

        But — so deeply red —
        some wounded petal from
        a window ledge?

        Came a second one,
        stigmata on a fustian sleeve,
        crimson rain, yes, blood,

God's tears, His oceanic repugnance.
So their curate spoke, watching
his abject flock implore heaven's mercy

                  on their souls.

Then one man, Pierese by name,
a fantasist, unpopular,
a flea under the soutane:
"Your miracle is butterfly merde."

Flammarion tells it straight:

        *A swarm of butterflies,*
        *leaving tree and field*
        *rose in clouds; their red*

*droppings spread panic*
*on the town of Aix*

O storm of powdered silk
too high to see, you swarmed
halfway round the world
                 from where — to where?

Nabokov's beloved nymphalid,
lepidoptera, hairy worm,
        true to your discipline
        as if obeying
        an ordained
        choreography of
        sublimity in transit.

Citizens of Aix! Look no further.
Your souls evanesce above you, scarlet
               tears of miraculous shit,

        prodigy enough
        for Monsieur Pierese
        (who, by the way,
        beat everyone at chess).

## RECKLESS WORDS

Though they are not lies they lie upon
the tongue like sticky doom on flies.

(He had not one cruel thought to his name,
the fly, so he was punished, so death came,

his agony spinning clockwise,
his buzz a roaring denial of wrongdoing.)


Though they are not flies, reckless words
can travel far in search of love or hate

with which to mate in brash midair.
Ebulliance rampant, somehow off-course,

they ricochet and zero in from ear to ear
and tongue to tongue, their paper wings

and foolish wits unable to prevent
crash landing on the tarmac of backyard.

# REMINDERS

Now the night barks like a dog
                the way it does when a dog barks
but don't let it delay departure —
                cut out before you change your mind
about the way to balance the bulge
                in your ancient luggage.

Bring without fail a nest egg for breakfast.
                Break the awful silence for lunch.
Bring me, bring me my dreaming lunch
                and my fairy godmother
cuddly as milk but unreliable.
                (She is not a fairy.)

Roll out my cities' red, high-piled carpets
                for would-be governments.
Raid an orphanage, grab an inmate.
                We'll compare our porcupine tea,
our notes on scorn rap-slapped at us
                in horizon-blue accents.

You might bring me a list of alibis,
                easy to carry in your pocket,
reading I can settle down with
                when the inquiry is started.
Oh, and things we'll need for our escape:
                the slow moon's cowl,

        the sudden stars.

## REPORT FROM THE FIELD

Sublimation, a new version of piety,
Hovers the paint and gets her going.
Everything drifts, a barely heard sigh is the

Sound of wind in the next room blowing
Dust from anxiety. A favorite receptacle
Holds her breath and occasional sewing.

Only the artist will be held responsible
For something so far unsaid but true,
For having the crust to let the hysterical

Earnest of genuine feeling show through,
And watching herself in the glassy eyeing
Of *Art as seen through a hole in her shoe.*

Painter and poet, sometimes said to be lying,
Agonizingly know it is more like dying.

# RUE MONGE NARRATED

Up or down it, disguise and
discretion go both ways.
Indifferent to tone,
peeling paint adds cachet:
patina proudly worn
as uniform.

Varnish sweats like skin
in the stair. Concierge
behind lace curtains
waits for deliverance.
Who cares if care has
stained her age?

Even spring is autumnal:
pallor of sun and leaf
on café table where
one tiny cup, thick and
white and brown inside,
is pushed aside

by occupant of wicker chair.
His notebook opened up,
he sees nothing much,
ballpoint hovering
like a copter over
the paper target.

Girl beside him out of
makeup like cement
looks round at nothing.
Oh, she has time, all
the time in the world
to be respectful

of whatever is on his page.
Yes, all this deadpan
afternoon yawns as, warm
and sleepy, she waits
to be wildly wildly
wanted later on.

# SECRET

On one of those birthdays of which I've had so many
I was walking home through the park from a party,

pleased that I'd resisted mentioning the birthday —
why hear congratulations for doing nothing but live?

The birthday was my secret with myself and gave me,
walking under all those trees, such a strong feeling of

satisfaction that everything else fell away: party sounds,
the hostess who stared and as suddenly disappeared

on seeing her husband walk in with a young(er) friend;
another guest examining garment labels in the room

where I went to leave my jacket; one of two waiters
balancing a trayful of foot-high champagne glasses;

a bee-like buzz of voices I ought to have enjoyed
but heard as foreign babble, so remote it was from

a birthday, so empty of import nothing would remain.
I got my jacket, waved from the hall, pressed *Down*.

In summer the park, for an hour or so before night,
is at its greenest, a whole implicit proposition

of green leaves, a triumph of leaves enfolding me
that day in a green intimacy so trustworthy I told

them my secret: "It's my birthday," I said out loud
before turning away to cross the avenue.

# SEQUESTRIENNE

Don't look at me
for answers. What am I but
a sobriquet,
a teeth-grinder,
grinder of color,
and vanishing point?

There was a time
of middle distance, unforgettable,
a sort of lace-cut
flame-green filament
to ravish my
skintight eyes.

Heaven's motes sift
to salt white — paint is ground
to silence; and I,
I am bound, unquiet,
a shade of blue
in the studio.

If it isn't too late
let me waste one day away
from my history.
Let me see without
looking inside
at broken glass.

## SIBYLLINE

The noisy season takes its toll in fearfulness,
looking over the shoulder, days of digging in
concrete cocoons for unlit, careful weekends,

for a time not quite imagined, when dearth is
a name for earth: this place where all you have
to make is war to vanish from its face, as did

those colorful mastodons and peoples we like
to read about: their bones, fragments, ruins
for visiting, legends researched to death, as

death it was for them — not one at a time with
sad funerals but all at once, their primal lore
now rendered in lifelike plastic to intrigue

our screaming children, keep them busy and
out of the way while we don our battle dress.

# SIX AVIAN PERILS

### I

If his juvenile behavior appalls,
if the word bird has three toes,
if its message is heard in
the driest of grasses

while he slips through steel
only to succumb to her arrow,
then look for him up
at the fortune-teller's pad.

Both of them lolling on
fog-embroidered cushions;
both of them entwined,
pearl hammock swung

between flight and frenzy;
both of them clinging to the ages.
Pensive, they tear up a pack
of cards, stuff them in the mattress.

Fifty-two cards and joker —
the one they had disdained.
Look: downed in a perfect vertical,
they lie in a pool of ooze.

### II

I'm a high flyer.
My sarcastic colors pack no bags.
Reality grounds my neighbors —
from inadvertence to inadvertence,
from my music to their chemical menu
they miss the point.

They marvel as, upside-down,
I roll away. In three ellipses,
one radiant exaggeration, I catch
at Zeno's arrow. Come — I offer you
the haven of my pure wing.

(a short silence)

So long, earth. So long, walls.


**III**

                But
have you seen my boy
in his magnetic field?
Red plastron, dolent crest —
just to see him turn his head,
the incredible precision —
diving, his trajectory
leans seventy degrees.
He tricks the tempest,
laughs at storms with teeth,
hangs no-hands on ether.

*Where am I?*
*Should I pretend*
*to an equilibrium?*

Birdance, birdeath.
Oh my boy. . . .

*Do I have to stop dancing?*

(Carry a keyhole,
the only way to surprise him.)


## IV

April-dyed gauze intertwined
is spring in Marrakech.

This year's wing across the Pamirs,
the secret stopover at Salonika,

have swollen his lungs.

He holds the terrestrial rind,
ponders perfection. He gets well.

Deploying spills of saliva
he crochets his nest in zigzags.

There the bride, opal-necklaced,
comes to lay her perfect egg.


## V

My fiancé is a concept. An appearance.
Behind my fiancé are cage bars.
He touches the bars with his long

varnished feet, music in shards
bring out the essence of my fiancé,
all striped as he is.

Give him the clock and the hour.
He'll hang in there, play his flute,
rap out our naïve conceptions.

His cry dangles between roofs
and ochre haze. . . an alarm.
Schoolgirls report him:

savage eye, torn collar, haggard beak.
Crowds. Gunshot. The roofs retreat
in fast forward. To the barricages!

Why blame flaming schoolgirls?
His cage is roofless, empty.
Blind bars, blackened mirror.

His itinerary slices at the wind.
He loses altitude, head bowed
a little to the left as the flower
bows, heavy with bees,

his dream upending.


## VI

Our parabolas drape their fringe
in viper-bitten air. We write
a tale of vapor, our flight line
stolen, lost, or fallen

asleep to wake or not.
Old sky gone snakeskin dry.
Oh we're wild to slice the air,
wild to singe our wings.

# SPACE DISARMED

*(for Merce Cunningham)*

When   5 barely believable
        bodies
           become
      1 thought;

when in
      1 endless instant
        they bring
          beginning and
end of their
      separateness to

      1 idea and its outcome,

      1 intrigue
        and its unraveling

and if, by chance,

      1 chance operation
        springs unbidden
        onto
        your open design,
like a tiger into a clearing;

then,
      in that moment,

transcendence is perceived
      by our
        caught
          breath.

# STRAWBERRIES

*Waiting in line for the bus that never comes*
*In winter rain. A long line waits at the bank*
*For money. A line inches up to the post office*
*Stamp window (fresh out of new stamps).*

At last at the supermarket, I wait like the others
In several lines; and I ask myself: how many
Of the people in them are as patient as they look.
I for one am not in any hurry. I feel righteous

And kindly, almost levitating as I move among
All that bounty. You wouldn't believe my sweet
Self-control as I reach for that last box of straw-
Berries and someone grabs it from behind.

I just smile to myself and push on to my next
Indifference, my next invincibility, my ever calm
But scratchy shift away from things quotidian,
Sidestepping on the fresh-produce aisle floor

A little pile of spilled strawberries being angrily
Trampled by a shopper. He stamps and pivots
In the wet mess with hostile attention, staring
At the berries as if they were bugs or slugs.

Standing in line at checkout I watch the checker
Slip a strawberry from the cash drawer and pop
It in her mouth while making change. Red juice
Is running down her chin and onto her shirt.

The wonder is, no one but me appears to notice
The stains — city people are so inured to anything
And everything but at least they ought to show
Some surprise if not the dizziness that's drawing

This reddish film over my sorely tried indifference
As all these people begin throwing strawberries
At each other or just into the air like children with
Snowballs in a frenzy of foolishness, the disgraceful

Bloodstains all over them certain to be noticed
Once they're out in the street, my steady unconcern
Shattering as I emerge and a woman points in horror
At me dripping in a red puddle of equanimity.

# SYBARIS

Siesta breathes in the old plane trees,
veterans of annual amputation:
witness their knots and knobs.

Up here the house is tight.
Summer's out listening to locusts
rub their ceaseless one-note instrument.

A single leaf lolls on the blue pool.
My dog's eyes tell me I'm powerful.
The windows glitter with landscape,

walls are thick with books and pictures,
the cellar is rich, the garden is rich,
the guest is richly suntanned.

What is it then that is grieving?
My thought is poor, my words are poor,
my brain is whitening by the hour,

a see-through brain and, look —
what is that awful spot on the floor?
Why is it widening, crowding me?

# IV

---

**T to W**

# THE TRIUMPH OF VENUS

"Curl up on my petal-bed.
Its spore is just the dust
You hanker for.

Try my orgiastic seed
To actuate your dreams.
I'll be your bride.

Breathe me! Oh, I permeate,
Inebriate. I suffocate.
Can you, this once,

Observe me as my weed
Casts its spell on what
You call your soul?

Look — I'll make a trade:
My sepal's mesh for
Nothing but your wings."

At this he drank, gloated:
*"Imagine: a flying flower"* . . .
He drank deep,

Five petals closing over
Him, wings crimpled
In thickest pollen.

# THIS IS A RECORDING

girls
silk-slippered and yawning
among whitest of lies,
they linger —
hair exploding
on impact in the
chiffonades,
quiet as stage snow,
no one in pain.

boys
spaced-out and speeding
round for a ride blow
hot-rod ruin,
saturday skin on fire,
ready to spin
nets of gas-choke
and shift one-handed;
no one is hurt.

other
people into winning and,
alas, losing,
desire and
disquiet hidden
under hair or none
silently screaming
the question without
an answer.

# TIME FLEW

*(2 hrs. 10 min.)*


Flurries, flurries
Dusting the flustered street.
Drifts rose.
He thought of red poppies.

Two flights up;
The bell the spell. The air
Was blue.
Some words fell on the rug.

She did
Her best — all politesse
At chess.
A king, a queen, checkmate.

Lifting,
Four eyes met in a blaze,
What they saw
Would have no end, both knew.

# TO OUR FATHER WHO ART

Hi, Dad,
We've never talked. You may not want to discuss your creative life
or address our yawning gulf, I mean the one that separates our statures,
yours and mine.

Oh, I always knew you were my biological father, I'm grateful for all
you've done, and if I've felt unfairly small you're quick to remind me
of my siblings

most of them invisible to the naked eye: uncomplaining, perfectly
programmed little components of order, they fit your stratagem —
enjoyed by all save

the ones made like me, their minds (of a sort) bent on changing yours.
Dad, you've seen the way your master plan has gotten out of sync
despite your warning

signs, writ large in air, waterways and fire — fire Prometheus surely
could not have intended — to say nothing of the hordes, the hordes.
As for the ones

like me, maybe you don't care, but if you have other plans —
I know you could, and even might, blow down this family tree —
I'd like to know,

though of course it wouldn't matter. Not at all. And by the way,
hey, thanks! Your patience helps me scrawl in black as I check out:
For Sale, Real Haunted House.

Your loving daughter.

## TO THAT GARDEN

When we are taken
there is a *with*
and a full flooding.
Incontinent rains come
on their way south, delivering silver mail.

If clouds had not parted,
if you had not loved me
in that garden —
rain spilling
its glassy wine on blue grapes

on musked melons —
as, uncomprehending,
our open mouths
gasped in the inebriate wet —
dark this time of night, drunk with sucked

rain ending too soon
for a dry throat,
for a body's rage; then
I could revile the rampant
growing of things all night long in the dark,

I might even
forget myself
and let my solitude
strangle the ghosts of
that garden, my phlox, your thorn.

# TOUR DYNAMICS

To lean on gray battlements
            under a matching sky where,
across a gray-walled courtyard
            and cobbled square,
            café tables patiently
            wait for us.

Someone tosses a pebble — stone?
            (every tour has its joker) —
down to where a gray cat
            plays with her kitten —
            little gray spot that
            moves no more,
the cat uttering a cry
            too small, too far away.

*No, no, not us — did I read it somewhere?*

Tired but true centuries in hoary staccato
dates details, rolling backward in their
            inconsequence.
Oriel slits of light, stale air, hollowed
stone stairs wind to the *pièce de résistance:*
a torture chamber so rich in ingenuity,
so vain in efficacy —
            iron gauntlet,
            wheel, rack —
            and an odd contraption
            for a man to stand
            inside it, iron spikes
            lining its heavy door
worked by a rope somewhere;

until our clown, he of the perfect aim,
                        shows us how it fits.
The door bangs shut,
                        a gray cat hangs from the rope.

*No, not our tour, not our clown stepping*
*back, grinning, as the guide barks, "Don't touch."*

## TO ZENO

You with your equation,
an arrow plugs your heart,
half in half out
makes nowhere at all.

You won't admit it
but what's left is time:
a patient sponge to stop
your arrow from bleeding.

It isn't more years I want,
just some older days.
If a day had four hours more
I think I could handle it.

My flightless friend, I'm waiting.
(We haven't all night.)
Burn up your dotted line.
Deck me out in minutes.

# TWO CITY MICE

This is the hour for getting back to where I'm supposed to be.
Call me, talk to me, I am yours. I am interested in what
You have to say, (if it's for me). Don't think I haven't tried
To fit the mold you've squeezed me in — after all, it isn't glass
And sizes are more realistic now. I've been away too long,

Too far, too. Not to worry. My empathy, my need for you
Is long secured. To be honest, I dote on you, I crave your talk.
You're there to keep me anchored to this life, this space I'm in
That tolerates me as I tolerate my resident mouse,

My rodent *semblable,* my tiny *frère.* "Tell me," I say to him,
"How you lived when curiosity drove me so far away,
When the phone and doorbell rang and nobody was home.
Who bought your cheese?" Oh, he would answer if he could.

Silence hears me telling him just about everything I can:
That much of what I once thought great I now repudiate;
That even though I feel some pride in what I do and did,
I am not one to overestimate achievement.

I want the chance to tell you things, the wilder the better —
Such as: how you have become my bandage and my wound;
Such as: though I cannot play you are my piano keyboard,
My spiral staircase, my prison without bars, my dot-com.

Between bouts of sublimation I stuff the airless maw
Of my malaise with wild oats harvested on the sly.
They're out of focus. Fax me now. Too late for a letter.
My mouse is not enough for me, he can't expect to be.
This is your hour. I'm waiting in this hole I occupy.

# UNFOUNDED CERTITUDES

If, waiting for you to begin,
    It's been there all along;
    If all you know is next time
And now the sky caves in;

If, say, you're caught between,
    And it's time to come to grief,
    Why wait your turn in line
Just for the end of the thing?

If in your down-filled shroud,
    Wellsprings actually leak,
    And fear itself is punctured
Like your present mood;

If a certain savagery persists;
    If by now you're shorn of skin
    And would welcome any fix,
Then all hail, walk in on this:

*Irrational reasons have made you think*
*Tomorrow's a crass and faceless place.*
*Come in, sit down, lock up the night.*
*Something will happen. Play your ace.*

# WAVERLY AND A PLACE

*(for Richard Howard)*

The room — a cave,
an Alexandria before the flames —
bound in boundlessness, a tapestry
of whispers, threads dangling

        on tenses

distinguishing the naked ear.
*What is this place, where am I here?*
Syntax lights the lamp; it's dark outside.
Voices like down insist, insist

        we are adrift.

It's anything you want, this galaxy
of prodigals in fabled seasons.
Our presence: invasion of privacy?
Waverly, serene, defines the evening

        of its Place.

You could think of Babel's tower. Yet
so much fervor, captive now,
breathes mesmerizing quietude:
reams of leaves in which to drown

        our panic.

A chime. It's late. Slant rain has
turned to snow. Time to go.
Speak for us, angels and demons of Parma
or Paris, Oran, Harar, Peking or

        Kathmandu —

islands, all islands, separate as we
who, shifting with tectonic tides,
merge, turn a cheek, a phrase,
leave this evening's alchemy —

                Away!

# WINDOW TREATMENT

My windows are private-eyed. They gape with authority:
what to let in, what to let out. Nothing dampens their zeal.

I can treat them as the void, fill them with landscape,
curtain them, hide from them, close them, nail them up.

Nothing fazes them. They let the sun in and they
shut night out; they bring something so far unbidden

to bear on my violent uncertainty — gasping with what
to let in, not sure what to keep out; while all along

I could spare myself the trouble, my indifferent windows
superbly keeping me in, waiting me out.